"Hey, we've lived every word of those fun cattle drives. We've been a part of them many times. 'Whoopee!' Try it sometime! You'll like it! Highly recommended!"
—Elmer and Jean McNeil,
Cattle Rancher and Lady Wrangler

(Note: since this endorsement was written I would like to acknowledge the passing away of my dear friend and trail boss, Elmer McNeil, with love and sympathy to Jean and her family. – Bobbie Smith)

"A fascinating collection of one liners and short poems showing the deep and personal side of the author, combined with the wit and humor of the cartoonist. Three cheers for this wonderful collection."
—Ron Nelson, Capa Lodge Trading,
American Indian Art & Crafts

"This book lets you see into the true heart of a cowgirl, and helps you understand how we really think."
—Rondel Holton, All-around teenage cowgirl

Cowgirl Up!

An American Cowgirl's Poems, True Stories & One-Liners

by **Bobbie Smith**
The Shady Lady

Robert D. Reed Publishers
San Francisco, California

Robert D. Reed Publishers
750 La Playa Street, Suite 647
San Francisco, CA 94121
Phone: 650/994-6570 • Fax: 650/994-6579
E-mail: 4bobreed@msn.com
Web site: www.rdrpublishers.com

Designed and typeset by Katherine Hyde
Cover designed by Julia A. Gaskill at Graphics Plus

ISBN 1-885003-86-2

Library of Congress Control Number: 2001088124

Produced and Printed in the United States of America

Special thanks to
Mary Katherine McMahon,
for without her help, support, and
encouragement I never could have
finished or even attempted
to write this book.

Contents

"No, no! I said this riding class would be goin' on a *night* ride, not a *knight* ride!"

Introduction

Take a 57-year-ol' cowgirl who grew up in Southern California . . . move her to Nevada . . . have her spend twenty years there . . . add eight failed marriages to that (move over Liz) . . . then let her live happily ever after on her ranch in northern Utah . . .

I've been asked several times why I had to marry all of the men I dated. My answer has always been, "I didn't. Only a small handful of them." I guess I kept tryin' to find one that was man enough to keep me. And I didn't.

Along with all these husbands, I've had several occupations: casino promoter, dog groomer, telephone operator, telephone lineman, secretary, bartender, cocktail waitress, hotel maid, casino girl, carhop, waitress, cook, etc., etc., etc. . . .

But through all these occupations and husbands, the one thing I've always been is a cowgirl. Cowgirl through and through. From stable owner to wrangler, if it had to do with a horse I was part of it. To my knowledge I was the first person to contract with UCLA to offer horsemanship classes. That was in 1962–63.

I walked away from my first stable, the Rafter R Ranch, for the name of love and a cowboy. Six months later I was doin' maid work at the Sands Motel in South Tahoe,

California, broke and pregnant. So much for cowboys . . .

After my son was born I went to work as a cocktail waitress at Sahara Tahoe (aka drink-packin' Barbie doll). That is where I met and married my bartender husband, number 5. That lasted two years . . .

So there I was, broke with another baby. Ended up in Reno, Nevada, at the Holiday Hotel as a cocktail waitress. So much for bartenders . . .

This is where I met husband number 6. Town playboy and casino promoter. My mother's boyfriend bet me I would never marry him. I bet him we would be married by the Fourth of July. I won the bet. We got married on June 29. That marriage lasted two years . . .

Husband number 7. Like an idiot I married this one twice. Mister power company lineman and motorcycle race promoter. What a joke. We were married for over ten years. In that time I went from secretary to telephone operator to lineman for Nevada Bell. Ten years with that man is a book in itself . . .

Now husband number 8. The firefighter. The only reason I married him was because my mother wanted me to. Her reason was so she wouldn't have to worry about me anymore. In the two years we were married I had gone from Nevada to Utah to California and back to Utah. When he left me he took our money, credit cards, and savings. That again is another story . . .

Then I shared my life with my old friend of thirty-eight years. We were together because he didn't try to change me. I lived six months of the year at his home in Southern California and the other six months at my ranch in Northern Utah, wranglin' cattle in the summer and doin' lunch in the winter.

Now, add all my life together and take a look at the humorous side of it. *Cowgirl Up!* is made up of different sayin's and experiences that I have heard or used or that have been a part of me throughout my life. The cartoons were drawn by my friend and companion, Ernest (Clide) Prete, Jr.

Now you know a little about the Shady Lady, and if you want to know more just ask me in person or read the book.

Happy readin'!

Bobbie Smith
The Shady Lady

The Shady Lady's Definition of "Cowgirl Up"

"Cowgirl up" is to gather up your reins and take control of any situation. To be strong and able to confront any obstacle that may get in your way—physically or mentally.

The
Cowgirl
Way

Cowgirl, Cal-Girl, or Ca-Girl

Cowgirl: A female ranch worker that herds cattle.

Cal-girl: A girl from California.

Ca-girl: A girl that dresses like a cowgirl but couldn't tell the front end from the back end of a horse or cow.

It's smarter to barter.

Ask a cowgirl.

She'll tell you it's so!

You're gonna like the way a cowgirl says thank you much better than the way she says please!

To judge another cowboy
will only give that cowboy
the right to judge you.

If you're gonna run with the big dogs, honey, you can't piddle like a pup!

You know you've had a
bad day when you look like
you've been rode hard and
put away wet!

Cowgirls are like young fillies. You gotta handle 'em with a light hand and a loose rein, and give 'em plenty o' room to run!

If a cowgirl's gonna survive in this ol' world, honey, she's gotta do what she's gotta do!

Someone once told me that cowgirls don't have any class. Well, honey, cowgirls have style, and when you have style you don't need class!

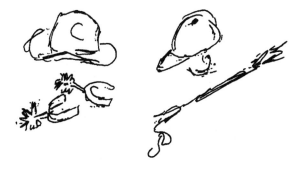

The next time you're caught out in the rain without an umbrella, remember one thing, honey. You're a cowgirl. You're not made of sugar and you're not gonna melt!

Goin' shoppin' with a
cowgirl is like playin'
cavalry with
General Custer.
She'll fill her hands with
credit cards and holler,
"Charge!"

A young child once
asked me if there were
horses in heaven.
My answer could only be,
"Of course! You couldn't
call it heaven without
horses!"

An ol' cowboy once
told me that the outside of a
horse was good for the
inside of a man.
Well, honey, it may be good
for the soul, but it can sure
make the body ache!

I'll never forget the day I was teachin' a group of six-year-olds a ridin' class at the Rafter R Ranch. One of the students noticed a mare and a stallion breedin' and said to me, "Miss Bobbie! Miss Bobbie! Look! That horse is getting a free ride!"

𝓐nytime I come across a person walkin' when I'm ridin' my horse I love to tell 'em, "If the good Lord wanted ya to walk, he'd 'a' never made a horse!"

$\mathcal{W}$hat's so great about
a cowgirl steppin' in a pile
of warm horse dung?
She knows a horse can't be
too far away!

As a young girl I was a car-
hop at a local drive-in restaurant
called The Country Burger.
We wore little cowgirl outfits.
I used to love it
when customers would ask me
where my horse was.
One of my favorite answers was,
"You're eating it!"
My other favorite answer was,
"Well, the front's tied up out back
and I'll give ya one guess as to the
part I'm talkin' to now!"

A cowgirl's handshake
on a deal is as good or
better than any contract
you may ask her to sign!

Take all the bull out of a six-foot cowboy and you'll end up with a foot and a half of cowboy hat, a belt buckle, and a pair of boots.

Wanna know why
cowboys wear bandanas
across their face
in the winter?
They do it so you can't see
the buggers running down
their moustache!

$\mathcal{C}$owboys perspire,
horses sweat,
and cowgirls dew!

$\mathcal{H}$oney, he may look
like a cowboy.
And he may talk like a cowboy.
But don't you call him a
cowboy 'til you see him ride!

What makes a cowboy?

Honey, he may walk the walk.

And he may talk the talk.

He may have the chaps, spurs,

and cowboy hat.

He may have a quarterhorse

and even dance the two-step.

But honey, if being a cowboy

isn't in his heart and soul,

he ain't ever gonna be a

cowboy, and sugar,

this cowgirl oughta know!

30

Cowboys are like
diamonds. They usually
come with a few flaws, and
at times it's hard to tell the
real thing from the fake!

Don't Tell Me the Good Lord Doesn't Watch Over Dudes!

Did you ever see the way a dude saddles a horse and then gets on and tries to ride it?

The bridle's so long the bit is about to fall out of the horse's mouth and tied on the horse's head in a way you could never dream of! The saddle blanket is about to fall off the back of the horse . . . if there is a blanket . . . The saddle cinch is so tight it cuts off the horse's breathin' . . . or so loose the saddle is only on by the grace of God. And of course the cinch strap is tied up in a way you've never seen before.

The amazin' part is when they ride up with the saddle stirrups six inches too short and they're tryin' to hold onto the reins and the horn at the same time! I never did figure out how they steered or stopped the darn horse!

*N*ever let a dude
unsaddle your horse.
It's amazin' to see how
many straps they can undo
and drag in the mud!

$\mathcal{I}$f I had my neighbor's
4×4 dual-E pickup truck
(aka: Cowboy Cadillac)
and he had a feather up his
butt, we'd both be tickled!

I've often heard that if a cowboy spit in one hand and wished in the other, the only thing he'd end up with is a handful of spit!

An ol' cowboy once told me that 1996 was such a dry year in Utah that the trees were chasin' the dogs!

Remember, when a cowgirl wants to walk she'll say "walk." When she says "whoa" you can bet she means stop!

A cowgirl's home is
like a mirror.
It's gotta be of her image.
Without her image,
it's not a home at all.
It's only a shell around her.

Curtains Up the Shady Lady Cowgirl Way!

Don't throw away those old horseshoes! They make great curtain hangers! From the tack room to the home. A real attention-getter and easy to make!

Usin' three horseshoe nails per shoe, nail one side of the shoe to the upper corner of the window, leavin' half of the shoe stickin' out and the other half bein' nailed to the inside of the window frame.

Repeat on the other side. Drape the material or a curtain rod through the inside part of the shoe sticking out. You can also attach a horseshoe to one side of a small thin piece of wood with an "L" bracket on the back. Use the bracket to attach to the center of the window frame.

Now you can drape your material behind the wood, getting the swag effect.

I just love the new bird-dog bras. You know, the ones that make pointers out of sitters!

It's a sure thing that a
cowgirl is gettin' old when
she looks down at her legs
and she realizes
the skin on her legs is also
lookin' down.
Or someone says her nylons
are saggin' and she ain't
wearin' any!

What happens to a cowgirl's body? Well, let me tell ya. I always figur'd my body was like a plum! Just as I started to mature I was green and hard. Then I got a little older and a little softer and sweeter. Now I'm turnin' into a wrinkled-up old prune!

Life on the Range

I'm Sure the Good Lord Don't Call It Cussin' When You're Wranglin' a Herd of Cattle

I'm sure the Good Lord don't call it cussin' when you're
    wranglin' a herd of cattle.
You know the kind I'm talkin' about.
They don't stay on a trail or out of the trees.
And oak brush seems to be their favorite place to be.
There's nothing like a hot summer's day
For them bovine to try your patience in every way.
I've renamed them cattle many a name, from body parts to
    family members.
Even the son of a dog and a few I won't mention.
If you ever wrangled cattle you know what I'm sayin'.
Them words you're hollerin' ain't nothing like prayin'!

On the Wings of a Bird

It was durin' the fall round-up in the Rocky Mountains of Utah. The ranchers and wranglers had been roundin' up cattle since daybreak. It was near noon so we decided to take a break and have a little lunch and give the cattle a rest at the same time.

Ol' Elmer pulled out a baloney sandwich for himself and a nice big fried-up piece of hamburger for his wife's dog, Lady. Comparin' the two lunches, Elmer made it very clear that when he died he wanted to come back as that dog. He figured she took better care of Lady than she did him.

After hearin' this ol' Don Wright said that when he met his maker he wanted to come back as a bird. We all laughed and never thought much more about what he had said. That is, not 'til a couple of years later. Ol' Don had gotten ill and up and passed away on us.

Gatherin' cattle just didn't seem the same after that. We had lost a good friend and cowboy. Don hadn't been gone a month when we were back on the mountain movin' cattle from one range to another.

Five other wranglers and myself were ridin' back to our trucks. Two by two, in three rows, along with two dogs that were walkin' between us.

Then out of the clear blue sky came a strange-lookin' bird. That crazy bird flew right through the center of us. It made a big circle, came back to the first two horses and walked between them.

Then he flew in another circle, came back and walked between the next two horses. He did the same to the last pair of horses. Durin' all this time the dogs kept walkin' between us. One of the wranglers said, "Look at that crazy bird!"

That is when I replied, "That ain't just any bird! Ol' Don Wright was ridin' on those wings!" And at that very moment that beautiful bird up and flew away.

Now think as you may, but I will always believe that ol' Don came back and wrangled cattle with us that day, and then on the wings of that very special bird he up and flew away . . .

The Good Lord's Snubbin' Post

I've been wranglin' cattle in the Rockies for many a year and one of the funniest things I ever saw was on the day we were checkin' cattle on the mountain. We rode up on two cowboys. It was ol' Elmer and Wayne. They had just roped a bull for doctorin'.

Now Wayne must weigh close to 250 to 300 pounds, a big-bellied man, dark hair, wearing a pair of those chink chaps that come just below the knee. Now take a thousand-pound bull, a 250-pound cowboy and an open flat of sagebrush, and you can bet the fun is just about to begin!

You see Wayne wasn't on a horse. He was runnin' behind the old bull. Elmer roped it. Wayne had to hold it. That bull took off across the flat with Wayne a-holdin' onto the rope.

Each step Wayne took got longer and longer as his chaps got lower and lower. Now picture this fat cowboy with his chaps dropped down to his knees, just a-flappin' in the breeze, as the bull pulled him up, over, under, and through the sagebrush. Not a tree in sight to dally a rope on . . .

I was laughin' so hard the tears were runnin' down my face as I hollered, "Hey, Wayne, how you gonna stop that ol' bull? That sagebrush ain't gonna do you much good. It won't hold 'em!"

I no more got them words out of my mouth and lo and behold there was a snubbin' post right there in the path of that ol' bull.

I swear the Good Lord must've put it there and helped us save the day. You see, I've rode that trail for many a year and I never seen that snubbin' post until that very day.

The Cattle Drive

The rooster was crowin'.
It was dark outside.
The time had come to rise.
I had a cup of coffee and fed my horse.
It was time for the cattle drive.
I packed my lunch and saddled up.
I got ready for an all-day ride.
I grabbed my chaps and spurs and cowboy hat.
I was ready for the cattle drive.
I loaded my horse.
They said don't be slow.
And we trailered them up the old mountain road.
Once we got to the meetin' place
We were goin' to split up so we couldn't be late.
There were ten stock trailers all parked in a row,
With twenty cowboys and horses all ready to go.
It was time to start the cattle drive.
Sure hoped I was ready for the all-day ride.
We all split up in groups of five.
You couldn't believe where them critters would hide.
Up the mountain trails we'd go,
Through rocks and streams,

Quakin' aspen and snow,

Through bogs and creeks,

Up mountainsides,

We checked all the meadows and the old rock slide.

Well, we found them cattle and wouldn't you know,

We had our hands full back to the old mountain road,

Whoopin' an' a hollerin' down that narrow mountain path.

Cows were bellowin' after their calves.

I was turnin' calves runnin' through the trees

And watchin' for those that would kick you in the knees.

I even turned an ol' bull on a dare.

He would take you in a minute so you had to beware!

I was lookin' for strays on the go,

Checkin' beaver ponds and other waterin' holes,

Through brush and pines, duckin' branches on the go.

I sure was happy to see that old mountain road.

We were whoopin' an' a-hollerin' ridin' through the trees.

I had a good broke horse and she did it with ease.

We got them cattle to the old mountain road,

To the old broke corral and all ready to load.

Before you knew it, we were ten stock trailers travelin' down
    the road,

All loaded with cattle we'd found and the tired horses we'd
    rode.

Well, I made it through the cattle drive,

And let me tell you folks, it was one hell of a ride!

Winter Round-Up

Roundin' up those last few strays
Makes for long hard lonely days.
We've looked in every hidden place.
My horse is tired and my body aches.
Ol' man winter's comin' near.
That mountain's rough this time of year.
Snow and slush, wind and rain.
I'm chilled plum through and my brain's gone lame.
Hat's pulled down snug and drippin' wet.
Scarf's wrapped twice around my neck.
My hands are froze and so's my nose.
That's how winter round-up goes.

Brandin' Time

Vaccinate. Castrate. Tag and notch an ear.
Twitch a tail. Slam a chute.
Smells of burnin' calf hair in the air.
Spring has come.
The calvin's done.
Brandin' time is here.
Bawlin' calves
And bellowin' cows.
My favorite time of year.

God's Cathedral

Here in God's cathedral,
Atop the mountain high,
Where pine and quakin' aspen
Reach up to meet the sky,
The sound of hooves beneath me
On this narrow path I ride,
It's here I meet my Master,
Atop the mountain high.
The deer, the elk, the moose, and birds
Make up His congregation,
For here in God's cathedral
We are all of His creation.
'Tis the mighty hand of God that made
This beauty all around me,
And it's here in God's cathedral
Where He rides along beside me.
The flowing streams,
The wildflowers,
The meadow grass grows tall.
This cathedral of tranquility,
God's gift to one and all.

So You Wanna Be a Cowboy

So, you wanna be a cowboy.
Well, let me tell ya, son . . .
It's a lonely life you're headed for
And a poor one rolled in one.
Now, you gotta know an anvil
And hot iron through and through.
'Cuz if you can't shoe a horse, son,
That cowboy life ain't meant for you.
Ya see that shoein's gonna feed ya
When hard times hit and towns are new.
So if you really wanna be a cowboy, son,
Go light that forge and set that shoe!

After being on several buffalo
round-ups over the past few years,
the one thing I've learned is
buffalo are a lot like cowboys.
You can drive, wrangle, and herd 'em
anywhere they wanna go!

*Y*ou can tell it's a rough rodeo when the score is:

Bulls – 10
Cowboys – 0

Elk Huntin'

I spent five years huntin' elk. I laid in the mud and walked through snow up to my waist. I hunted mountaintops to meadows. I blew through a tube that looked like it belonged to my vacuum cleaner. And I've sprayed some nasty-smellin' stuff they call elk scent all over me.

The one thing I finally realized is that this cow-girl had been huntin' somethin' a lot smarter than she was!

After several years of wranglin' cattle, you can bet I've run across a few old bulls that I wouldn't mind seein' as road kill!

The Heart of a Cowgirl

A cowgirl's gotta
dream her own dreams,
climb her own mountains,
and find happiness within
herself before she can share
happiness with another.

How many times must a cowgirl find love before love finds and keeps her forever?

$\mathcal{C}$owgirls gather
strength from the arms of
the men they love.

It takes a real man to find the tears inside the heart of a cowgirl, and a better man than that to make them disappear.

I told my mama one day, "Men are like a fine pair of boots. I always like to try 'em before I buy 'em." That's when my mama asked me, "Well if that's so, honey, how many times have you been resoled?"

Ropin' a cowgirl's a lot
like ropin' a mountain lion.
You'd better cowboy up,
honey, 'cuz you can bet
you're gonna have
your hands full!

There are many different
types of cowboys.
There are cattlemen,
wranglers, ranch hands,
and rodeo riders.
If I had to choose any of
'em it wouldn't be a rodeo
rider, 'cuz they figur'
after eight seconds,
the ride's over!

*N*ot all cowboys are
mice studyin' to be rats.
Only the ones I've dated.

Huntin' a man is like
huntin' big game.
The work doesn't really
start 'til after you've
bagged 'em!

always considered
myself a lot like
Robin Hood.
I always dated the rich and
married the poor!

There's one thing every
cowboy should know.
If you can't afford a
cowgirl, don't ask for one!

You can't tell me that
cowboys are cheap!
I had one over thirty years
ago and let me tell ya'
honey, I'm still makin'
payments on him!

Marriage is like
anything else.
If it's broke and it can't be
fixed, then get rid of it
and find something that
does work.
One important thing.
Be sure you throw out the
old one before you go
lookin' for something new!

Once a cowgirl gives
her love to a cowboy, that
love is his forever!
She can't take it back or
give it to another.
For each love is new.
It can grow or it can die.
But it can't be traded from
one to another.

Grub's On!

I've spent half of my life tellin' cowboys I don't cook. When they find out I can, I just tell 'em I never said I couldn't, I just said I didn't! Cowgirls get to go out a whole lot more that way. And honey, that's the cowgirl way.

Shady Lady Shooters

2/3 shot of butterscotch schnapps
1/3 shot of rum

Put 2/3 shot of butterscotch schnapps and 1/3 shot of rum in a shot glass. Serve as a shooter on the rocks, straight up shaken in a martini glass, or just fill up your flask and take it on the mountain!

Shady Lady shooter! Cowgirl cocktail! Wets your whistle in the summer, warms your belly in the winter!

Tequila Shooters

Dash of salt
One shot of tequila
Wedge of lime

Hold the lime between your thumb and first finger of your left hand. Lick your hand just below your thumb and sprinkle salt over licked area. Now take a deep breath and exhale. Hold your breath as you lick the salt off your hand. Down the tequila and suck the lime wedge.

Remember: The secret is not to breathe until after you've sucked the lime! That's the cowgirl way!

Cowboy Biscuits 'n' Gravy

1-1/2 pounds good ol' country sausage
2 tbsp. flour
1 12-oz. can evaporated milk
1–2 cups water
salt and pepper to taste

Crumble up your sausage and throw it in a wrought-iron skillet. Fry it up in the pan 'til it's browned real good. Now, drain off all but two tablespoons of fat and add two rounded tablespoons of flour. Cook on medium low heat stirrin' constantly 'til flour mixture is brown and bubbly.

Remove from heat and add evaporated milk and 1 cup of water. Continue stirrin'. Return to heat and bring to a boil. Keep stirrin' as gravy thickens. Cook and stir for at least five minutes. Add more water if gravy gets too thick. Add salt and pepper to taste.

Serve over drop biscuits or bread of choice. Tastes real good with elk steaks and homegrown cackleberries.

About the Author

From her early days at the Hilltop Stables of South Central Los Angeles, to the Hacienda Stables of Las Vegas, to the Rafter R Ranch of Canoga Park, California, to the 102 ranch of Reno, Nevada, to the Rockin' TK Ranch of Moor Park, California, to the Shady Lady Ranch in Northern Utah, Bobbie Smith continues to live out her childhood cowgirl dream with her crooked-eared horse Joker and three-legged dog I-lean.

Bobbie wrangles cattle all summer for some of the local ranchers and is a volunteer for the U.S. Forestry Service. In appreciation of Bobbie's many years of dedication on the mountain, the Shady Lady Spring has recently been named in her honor.